Knock Knock Jokes

for kids

First published in Great Britain 1987 by Ward Lock Limited,
8 Clifford Street, London W1X 1RB, an Egmont company.

This edition published 2004 by Bounty Books,
a division of Octopus Publishing Group Ltd,
2-4 Heron Quays, London E14 4JP
Reprinted 2004, 2005, 2007 (Twice), 2008

ISBN 978-0-753708-78-1

Printed and bound in Dubai

Knock Knock Jokes
for kids

Bounty
BOOKS

Knock, knock.
Who's there?
Peg.
Peg who?
Peg your pardon, I've forgotten.

Knock, knock.
Who's there?
Tim.
Tim who?
Timpossible to tell you.

COR-
A NEW
PLANET!

Knock, knock.
Who's there?
Duke.
Duke who?
Duke come here often?

Knock, knock.
Who's there?
Una.
Una who?
You nursing a bad tooth?

Knock, knock.
Who's there?
Val.
Val who?
Val, you ought to know by now.

Knock, knock.
Who's there?
Sue.
Sue who?
Sooner or later, I'll tell you.

BOY—IT MUST BE A PLANET FULL OF JOKES

Knock, knock.
Who's there?
Sid.
Sid who?
'S idiotic, that's who it is.

Knock, knock.
Who's there?
Mary.
Mary who?
Mary Christmas to all our readers.

Knock, knock.
Who's there?
Lionel.
Lionel who?
Lie and' I'll tell lies too.

Knock, knock.
Who's there?
Winston.
Winston who?
Win some, lose some.

Knock, knock.
Who's there?
Selina.
Selina who?
So leaner meat is better for you.

Knock, knock.
Who's there?
Jim.
Jim who?
J'imagine I'm going to tell you.

Knock, knock.
Who's there?
Joe.
Joe who?
Joking apart, I've forgotten.

Knock, knock.
Who's there?
Joy.
Joy who?
J'oil your bike regularly?

Knock, knock.
Who's there?
Ken.
Ken who?
Ken't you guess?

Knock, knock.
Who's there?
Kim.
Kim who?
Kim up and see me some time.

Knock, knock.
Who's there?
Kit.
Kit who?
Kit out of here!

Knock, knock.
Who's there?
Len.
Len who?
Len me a fiver.

Knock, knock.
Who's there?
Melinda.
Melinda who?
Me lend a fiver? Not likely.

Knock, knock.
Who's there?
Liz.
Liz who?
Liz is just ridiculous!

Knock, knock.
Who's there?
Lynn.
Lynn who?
Linger a little longer.

Knock, knock.
Who's there?
Max.
Max who?
Max little difference who it is.

Knock, knock.
Who's there?
Maxie.
Maxie who?
Maximum with maxidad.

Knock, knock.
Who's there?
May.
May who?
Made your mistake in asking.

Knock, knock.
Who's there?
Meg.
Meg who?
Meg an omelette without eggs.

Knock, knock.
Who's there?
Guy.
Guy who?
Guy do you ask?

Knock, knock.
Who's there?
Patrick.
Patrick who?
Patrically an idiot.

Knock, knock.
Who's there?
Martha.
Martha who?
Ma thirsts for a cold lemonade.

Knock, knock.
Who's there?
Peter.
Peter who?
P to Z is the end of the alphabet.

Knock, knock.
Who's there?
Celia.
Celia who?
Seal your envelope with sticky tape.

Knock, knock.
Who's there?
Shirley.
Shirley who?
Shirley you've guessed?

Knock, knock.
Who's there?
Phillip.
Phillip who?
Fill her up with petrol.

Knock, knock.
Who's there?
Juno.
Juno who?
Juno what I know?

Knock, knock.
Who's there?
Michael.
Michael who?
My collection's better than yours!

Knock, knock.
Who's there?
Mona.
Mona who?
Mown a lawn for fifty pence.

Knock, knock.
Who's there?
Thora.
Thora who?
Thaw a cube of ice with hot water.

Knock, knock.
Who's there?
Margie.
Margie who?
Margie-rine or butter?

Knock, knock.
Who's there?
Douglas.
Douglas who?
Dug lashings of potatoes up.

Knock, knock.
Who's there?
Leopold.
Leopold who?
Leo poled his punt up river.

Knock, knock.
Who's there?
Amy.
Amy who?
Eh? Me and several others.

Knock, knock.
Who's there?
Annie.
Annie who?
Annie body here seen my dog?

Knock, knock.
Who's there?
Ben.
Ben who?
Ben to the cinema lately?

Knock, knock.
Who's there?
Alf.
Alf who?
All fares, please.

Knock, knock.
Who's there?
Earl.
Earl who?
Early enough for you?

Knock, knock.
Who's there?
Ella.
Ella who?
'Ell of a row going on.

Knock, knock.
Who's there?
Dora.
Dora who?
Dora funny face on the blackboard.

Knock, knock.
Who's there?
Clem.
Clem who?
Clem up and say something.

Knock, knock.
Who's there?
Bill.
Bill who?
Belonging to next door?

Knock, knock.
Who's there?
Beth.
Beth who?
Bether late than never.

Knock, knock.
Who's there?
Amos.
Amos who?
A most respected person.

Knock, knock.
Who's there?
Adam.
Adam who?
A damp squib on November 5th.

Knock, knock.
Who's there?
Emile.
Emile who?
A military escort

Knock, knock.
Who's there?
Marion.
Marion who?
Marry an idiot and repent at leisure.

Knock, knock.
Who's there?
Tessa.
Tessa who?
Tess a coin to decide it.

Knock, knock.
Who's there?
Anita.
Anita who?
A neater way of putting it.

Knock, knock.
Who's there?
Harry.
Harry who?
Harry on to my house.

Knock, knock.
Who's there?
Nat.
Nat who?
Nat going to tell you.

Knock, knock.
Who's there?
Pam.
Pam who?
Pamission granted.

Knock, knock.
Who's there?
Isabel.
Isabel who?
Is a belfry a batty place?

Knock, knock.
Who's there?
Eileen.
Eileen who?
I leaned over and fell.

Knock, knock.
Who's there?
Ida.
Ida who?
I'd a hoe but lost it in the garden.

Knock, knock.
Who's there?
Abel.
Abel who?
A bull and a cow had a row.

Knock, knock.
Who's there?
Nora.
Nora who?
Gnaw a bone if you have any teeth.

JUST MY—
I LEFT MY
FALSE TEETH
AT HOME

Knock, knock.
Who's there?
Walter.
Walter who?
Wall to wall carpet.

Knock, knock.
Who's there?
Robin.
Robin who?
Robin the rich to give to the poor.

Knock, knock.
Who's there?
Rosa.
Rosa who?
Rows a boat around the harbour.

Knock, knock.
Who's there?
Francis.
Francis who?
France is the other side of the channel.

Knock, knock.
Who's there?
Adam.
Adam who?
Add 'em or subtract 'em.

Knock, knock.
Who's there?
Aldo.
Aldo who?
All donations welcome.

Knock, knock.
Who's there?
Amos.
Amos who?
A mosquito is the same as a gnat.

Knock, knock.
Who's there?
Andy.
Andy who?
And 'e never said thank you.

Knock, knock.
Who's there?
Alan.
Alan who?
A lantern burning brightly.

Knock, knock.
Who's there?
Violet.
Violet who?
Vile it may be, if it's strong medicine.

Knock, knock.
Who's there?
Yvonne.
Yvonne who?
'Eave on that rope, lads!

Knock, knock.
Who's there?
Abigail.
Abigail who?
A big gale, or a storm in a teacup?

Knock, knock.
Who's there?
Barbara.
Barbara who?
Baa-baa black sheep.

Knock, knock.
Who's there?
Jessica.
Jessica who?
Je-seek a new boyfriend?

Knock, knock.
Who's there?
Milly.
Milly who?
Milliners may be mad as hatters.

Knock, knock.
Who's there?
Maxwell.
Maxwell who?
Mac's well but Annie's poorly.

Knock, knock.
Who's there?
Lucille.
Lucille who?
Loose 'eel and a worn out sole.

Knock, knock.
Who's there?
Lucinda.
Lucinda who?
Lou's in dirty surroundings.

Knock, knock.
Who's there?
Margaret.
Margaret who?
My regret for my mistake.

Knock, knock.
Who's there?
Solomon
Solomon who?
Solemn on this serious occasion.

Knock, knock.
Who's there?
Harriet.
Harriet who?
Hurry it along there.

Knock, knock.
Who's there?
Sarah.
Sarah who?
Sarah way out of this maze?

Knock, knock.
Who's there?
Christy.
Christy who?
Chris, tea or coffee?

Knock, knock.
Who's there?
Felicity.
Felicity who?
Fill a city with skyscrapers.

Knock, knock.
Who's there?
Benjamin
Benjamin who?
Been jammin' the blues?

Knock, knock.
Who's there?
Leon.
Leon who?
Leigh-on-Sea is near Southend.

Knock, knock.
Who's there?
Julie.
Julie who?
Ju-leak official secrets?

Knock, knock.
Who's there?
Ariadne.
Ariadne who?
'Arry 'ad next to nothing.

Knock, knock.
Who's there?
Adeline.
Adeline who?
'Ad a line of washing hanging out today.

Knock, knock.
Who's there?
Wyndham.
Wyndham who?
Wind 'im with a low blow.

Knock, knock.
Who's there?
Wallis.
Wallis who?
Well as can be expected.

Knock, knock.
Who's there?
Jeff.
Jeff who?
J-effer see such a sight?

Knock, knock.
Who's there?
Humphrey.
Humphrey who?
Hum free, but there's a charge for singing.

Knock, knock.
Who's there?
Rosalie.
Rosalie who?
Rose early and went to bed late.

Knock, knock.
Who's there?
Rebecca.
Rebecca who?
Rebuke 'er for such bad behaviour!

Knock, knock.
Who's there?
Justin.
Justin who?
Just in time for bed.

Knock, knock.
Who's there?
Vaughan.
Vaughan who?
Vorn out with over-vorking.

Knock, knock.
Who's there?
Madeline.
Madeline who?
Meddlin' and fiddlin' the books.

Knock, knock.
Who's there?
Yolande.
Yolande who?
Yo land at Gatwick from Spain?

Knock, knock.
Who's there?
William.
William who?
Will yam cook us up a vegetable?

Knock, knock.
Who's there?
Noah.
Noah who?
Know a better way of doing it?

Knock, knock.
Who's there?
Geoffrey.
Geoffrey who?
J-free that prisoner who was innocent?

Knock, knock.
Who's there?
Natalie.
Natalie who?
Naturlie, we're delighted to see you.

Knock, knock.
Who's there?
Lorraine.
Lorraine who?
Low rain in London.

Knock, knock.
Who's there?
Jock.
Jock who?
J-occupy all this house?

Knock, knock.
Who's there?
Jules.
Jules who?
Jewels and gems and semi-precious stones.

Knock, knock.
Who's there?
Maximillion.
Maximillion who?
Makes a millionaire look poor!

Knock, knock.
Who's there?
Wilhelmina.
Wilhelmina who?
Will Hell mean a fire in every room?

Knock, knock.
Who's there?
Nicolette.
Nicolette who?
Nick a letter and steam it open.

Knock, knock.
Who's there?
Rosemary.
Rosemary who?
Rose merry after a good night's sleep.

Knock, knock.
Who's there?
Wanda.
Wanda who?
Wanda new friend?

Knock, knock.
Who's there?
Rosie.
Rosie who?
Row secretly out of port.

Knock, knock.
Who's there?
Theodore.
Theodore who?
The odour is horrible.

Knock, knock.
Who's there?
Sybil.
Sybil who?
So billions of pounds are spent.

Knock, knock.
Who's there?
Jacquetta.
Jacquetta who?
Jack ate a sour apple and has tummy-ache.

Knock, knock.
Who's there?
Susie.
Susie who?
Sues easily when wronged.

Knock, knock.
Who's there?
Sonia.
Sonia who?
S' on yer own head, be it!

Knock, knock.
Who's there?
Simon.
Simon who?
So I'm on night-duty again.

Knock, knock.
Who's there?
Sandy.
Sandy who?
Sandy afternoon on the beach.

Knock, knock.
Who's there?
Sadie.
Sadie who?
Say, dear, if you've had enough.

Knock, knock.
Who's there?
Percy.
Percy who?
Persecuted for very little reason.

Knock, knock.
Who's there?
Pearl.
Pearl who?
Purr like a fat cat.

Knock, knock.
Who's there?
Ashton.
Ashton who?
Ash turned out of the grate.

Knock, knock.
Who's there?
Norma.
Norma who?
Nor Ma nor Pa nor Uncle Bill.

Knock, knock.
Who's there?
Norman.
Norman who?
Norman service will be resumed shortly.

Knock, knock.
Who's there?
Nelly.
Nelly who?
Nelly midnight, Cinderella.

Knock, knock.
Who's there?
Myrna.
Myrna who?
My nerves are shot to pieces.

Knock, knock.
Who's there?
Moira.
Moira who?
More a fool than a knave.

Knock, knock.
Who's there?
Mitzi.
Mitzi who?
Mid-sea romance and wedding.

Knock, knock.
Who's there?
Maria.
Maria who?
M'rear window is misted up.

Knock, knock.
Who's there?
Margo.
Margo who?
Mar go buy some shopping.

Knock, knock.
Who's there?
Madge.
Madge who?
Majority in favour.

Knock, knock.
Who's there?
Lidia.
Lidia who?
Lid o' yer teapot's cracked.

Knock, knock.
Who's there?
Kevin.
Kevin who?
Cave in under pressure.

Knock, knock.
Who's there?
Keith.
Keith who?
Key thief can unlock your door.

Knock, knock.
Who's there?
Joyce.
Joyce who?
Joyce of the orange without additives.

Knock, knock.
Who's there?
Aaron.
Aaron who?
'Air on chest means strength in arms.

Knock, knock.
Who's there?
Jerry.
Jerry who?
J'erect that extraordinary building?

Knock, knock.
Who's there?
Janet.
Janet who?
Janitors are the same as caretakers.

Knock, knock.
Who's there?
Jacqueline.
Jacqueline who?
Jekyll and Hyde.

Knock, knock.
Who's there?
Issac.
Issac who?
I suck my thumb when I'm bored.

Knock, knock.
Who's there?
Honor.
Honor who?
On a clear day, you can see forever.

Knock, knock.
Who's there?
Hiram.
Hiram who?
Hire 'em, fire 'em, don't pay 'em.

Knock, knock.
Who's there?
Hilda.
Hilda who?
He'll demand to know her name.

Knock, knock.
Who's there?
Helga.
Helga who?
He'll guard her with his life.

Knock, knock.
Who's there?
Helen.
Helen who?
Hell an' high water.

Knock, knock.
Who's there?
Grace.
Grace who?
Grey's the colour of warships.

Knock, knock.
Who's there?
Giles.
Giles who?
Child's play to get the answer.

Knock, knock.
Who's there?
Romeo.
Romeo who?
Row me over the river.

Knock, knock.
Who's there?
Juliet.
Juliet who?
Juliet him get away with that?

Knock, knock.
Who's there?
Portia.
Portia who?
Pour sherbet into a glass

Knock, knock.
Who's there?
Thea.
Thea who?
The early bird catches the worm.

YUM YUM - BREAKFAST

Knock, knock.
Who's there?
Ray.
Ray who?
Ray of sunshine.

Knock, knock.
Who's there?
Theo.
Theo who?
The Old Curiosity Shop.

Knock, knock.
Who's there?
Fred.
Fred who?
Fred this needle for me, please.

I HATE
HOMEMADE
PANTS

Knock, knock.
Who's there?
Gail.
Gail who?
Gail warning to all shipping.

Knock, knock.
Who's there?
Wendy.
Wendy who?
When d'you expect to see him?

Knock, knock.
Who's there?
Hugh.
Hugh who?
Huge reductions in all departments.

Knock, knock.
Who's there?
Hugo.
Hugo who?
You going away on holiday?

Knock, knock.
Who's there?
Iris.
Iris who?
Irish stew and dumplings.

Knock, knock.
Who's there?
Ivan.
Ivan who?
I've angered you again.

Knock, knock.
Who's there?
Jess.
Jess who?
Gesture of goodwill.

Knock, knock.
Who's there?
Joan.
Joan who?
Joan your own house?

Knock, knock.
Who's there?
Jess.
Jess who?
Jespect me to believe you?

Knock, knock.
Who's there?
Jude.
Jude who?
Judeliver newspapers still?

Knock, knock.
Who's there?
Colin.
Colin who?
Colanders are full of holes.

Knock, knock.
Who's there?
Lena.
Lena who?
Lean a bike against the wall.

Knock, knock.
Who's there?
Terry.
Terry who?
Terrible twins or tricky triplets?

Knock, knock.
Who's there?
Trixie.
Trixie who?
Tricks 'e plays on 'er.

Knock, knock.
Who's there?
Hamish.
Hamish who?
Hey, Mishter, ish thish the way to Shishester?

Knock, knock.
Who's there?
Charlie.
Charlie who?
Charlie that's not your boyfriend?

Knock, knock.
Who's there?
Bob.
Bob who?
Bobbin' up and down like this.

Knock, knock.
Who's there?
Evelyn.
Evelyn who?
Evelyn all!

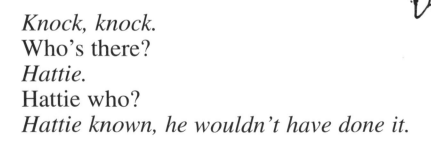

Knock, knock.
Who's there?
Hattie.
Hattie who?
Hattie known, he wouldn't have done it.

Knock, knock.
Who's there?
Gideon.
Gideon who?
Giddy on the swings and roundabouts.

Knock, knock.
Who's there?
Ronnie.
Ronnie who?
Ronnie butter spreads more quickly.

Knock, knock.
Who's there?
Dwight.
Dwight who?
Dwight or wrong?

Knock, knock.
Who's there?
Dougal.
Dougal who?
Do gulls nest on icebergs?

Knock, knock.
Who's there?
Eugene.
Eugene who?
You Jean or Joyce?

Knock, knock.
Who's there?
Carmen.
Carmen who?
Car men don't like walking.

THAT IS TWO NAUGHTY COPPER JOKES SO FAR - I ARREST THIS BOOK!

Knock, knock.
Who's there?
Arthur.
Arthur who?
Arthur loaf is better than none.

Knock, knock.
Who's there?
Bertha.
Bertha who?
Berth a boat in a dry dock.

Knock, knock.
Who's there?
Audrey.
Audrey who?
Ordering your meal now?

Knock, knock.
Who's there?
Archie.
Archie who?
Are cheese always round.

Knock, knock.
Who's there?
Arabel.
Arabel who?
A rabble of football supporters.

Knock, knock.
Who's there?
Claire.
Claire who?
Claire your throat before speaking.

Knock, knock.
Who's there?
Carrie
Carrie who?
Carry your bags, Mister?

Knock, knock.
Who's there?
Connor.
Connor who?
Connor long way past his turning.

Knock, knock.
Who's there?
Damian.
Damian who?
Day me and my mate went on holiday.

Knock, knock.
Who's there?
Denise.
Denise who?
Denise having anything to do with it.

Knock, knock.
Who's there?
Dermot.
Dermot who?
Dermatology is only skin deep.

Knock, knock.
Who's there?
Doreen.
Doreen who?
Door Ian slammed in my face.

Knock, knock.
Who's there?
Alison.
Alison who?
Alice on a bike is quite amusing.

Knock, knock.
Who's there?
Andrea.
Andrea who?
And rear view is of the open fields.

Knock, knock.
Who's there?
Aileen.
Aileen who?
A leaning tower is in Pisa.

Knock, knock.
Who's there?
Caesar.
Caesar who?
Caesar jolly good fellow.

Knock, knock.
Who's there?
Freda.
Freda who?
Freed 'er from prison.

Knock, knock.
Who's there?
Ava.
Ava who?
Ava good mind to leave.

Knock, knock.
Who's there?
Seth.
Seth who?
'S Ethel who's my sister.

ETHEL (LOVELY THING)

Knock, knock.
Who's there?
Cain.
Cain who?
Cain't you see through a brick wall?

Knock, knock.
Who's there?
Atlas.
Atlas who?
At Las Vegas you can gamble all night.

Knock, knock.
Who's there?
Grace.
Grace who?
Grey stones may be granite.

Knock, knock.
Who's there?
Minnie.
Minnie who?
Minestrone or mulligatawny soup for you?

Knock, knock.
Who's there?
Ethelred.
Ethelred who?
Ethel reddened when kissed.

SMART
ALEXANDER'S
SUPER
LONG-RANGE
LIPS

Knock, knock.
Who's there?
Moira.
Moira who?
Moiracles do happen.

Knock, knock.
Who's there?
Uriah.
Uriah who?
Uriah than I am in the ratings.

Knock, knock.
Who's there?
Apollo.
Apollo who?
A polo player.

Knock, knock.
Who's there?
Oberon.
Oberon who?
Oberon the other side of the road.

Knock, knock.
Who's there?
Aladdin.
Aladdin who?
A lad inspired to great deeds.

Knock, knock.
Who's there?
Pandora.
Pandora who?
Pan Dora fried the fish in.

Knock, knock.
Who's there?
Tristan.
Tristan who?
Tristan shout.

Knock, knock.
Who's there?
Alexander.
Alexander who?
Alec's under the doctor.

Knock, knock.
Who's there?
Jonah.
Jonah who?
Jonah bicycle?

Knock, knock.
Who's there?
Jupiter.
Jupiter who?
Jupiter strong man against a weak one?

Knock, knock.
Who's there?
Aesop.
Aesop who?
Aesop to his old tricks.

Knock, knock.
Who's there?
Christopher.
Christopher who?
Chris to offer a bargain.

Knock, knock.
Who's there?
Petronella.
Petronella who?
Pet, Ron, Ella, and anyone else who wants to go.

Knock, knock.
Who's there?
Job.
Job who?
Joe burped after every meal.

Knock, knock.
Who's there?
Lot.
Lot who?
Lot on your plate.

Knock, knock.
Who's there?
Ahab.
Ahab who?
A habit you want to break.

Knock, knock.
Who's there?
Jude.
Jude who?
Jude to unseen circumstances.

Knock, knock.
Who's there?
Luke.
Luke who?
Luke both ways before crossing.

Knock, knock.
Who's there?
Mark.
Mark who?
Ma can't cook for toffee.

Knock, knock.
Who's there?
Saul.
Saul who?
Saul over and done with.

STICK TO
BONES-MAN

Knock, knock.
Who's there?
Jimmy.
Jimmy who?
J'imitate TV personalities?

Knock, knock.
Who's there?
Enoch.
Enoch who?
Inoculated against everything.

Knock, knock.
Who's there?
Herod.
Herod who?
Hair oddly waved.

Knock, knock.
Who's there?
Hosea.
Hosea who?
Hosea and use the watering-can there.

Knock, knock.
Who's there?
Judas.
Judas who?
Judash about like that all the time?

Knock, knock.
Who's there?
Isaiah.
Isiah who?
Eyes 'igher with high-brows.

Knock, knock.
Who's there?
Silas.
Sila who?
Silas is golden.

Knock, knock.
Who's there?
Uriel.
Uriel who?
You real or unreal?

Knock, knock.
Who's there?
Micah.
Micah who?
My car goes faster than yours.

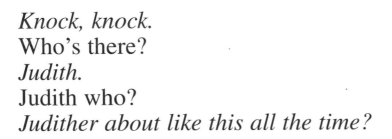

Knock, knock.
Who's there?
Judith.
Judith who?
Judither about like this all the time?

Knock, knock.
Who's there?
Samuel.
Samuel who?
Samuel keep, some you'll throw out.

Knock, knock.
Who's there?
Ephraim.
Ephraim who?
A frame for your photograph.

Knock, knock.
Who's there?
Matthew.
Matthew who?
Matthew always speak with that lisp?

Knock, knock.
Who's there?
Alonso.
Alonso who?
Alone so long, I talk to myself.

Knock, knock.
Who's there?
Angus.
Angus who?
Angus us to see such cruelty.

Knock, knock.
Who's there?
Antonio.
Antonio who?
An' Tony owed even more.

Knock, knock.
Who's there?
Archibald.
Archibald who?
Archie bald, but Arthur wears a wig.

Knock, knock.
Who's there?
Blanche.
Blanche who?
Blanche-manager turned very pale.

Knock, knock.
Who's there?
Cressida.
Cressida who?
Cress 'id her feet under a cushion.

Knock, knock.
Who's there?
Curtis.
Curtis who?
Courtesy is a sign of a good upbringing.

Knock, knock.
Who's there?
Elizabeth.
Elizabeth who?
I lose a bet every time I back a horse.

Knock, knock.
Who's there?
Owen.
Owen who?
Owen up, you did it.

Knock, knock.
Who's there?
Ellen.
Ellen who?
Elementary, my dear Watson.

Knock, knock.
Who's there?
Katharine.
Katharine who?
Katharine together for a social evening.

Knock, knock.
Who's there?
Macbeth.
Macbeth who?
Macbether now, thank you.

Knock, knock.
Who's there?
Martin.
Martin who?
Martin of sweets has gone.

Knock, knock.
Who's there?
Clifford.
Clifford who?
Cliff ordered jelly and got trifle.

Knock, knock.
Who's there?
Russel.
Russel who?
Rustle up a few more people.

Knock, knock.
Who's there?
Talbot.
Talbot who?
Tall but too thin

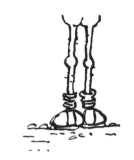

Knock, knock.
Who's there?
Lucy.
Lucy who?
Loose elastic can let you down.

Knock, knock.
Who's there?
Lucetta.
Lucetta who?
Lou set a difficult question.

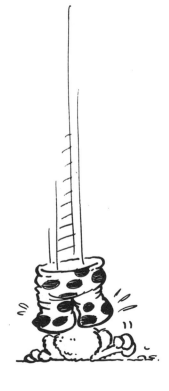

Knock, knock.
Who's there?
Lysander.
Lysander who?
Lies – and only a few are white ones.

Knock, knock.
Who's there?
Marcus.
Marcus who?
Marcus in, I've forgotten my pen.

Knock, knock.
Who's there?
Natasha.
Natasha who?
Not a shirt I'd wear.

Knock, knock.
Who's there?
Mariana.
Mariana who?
Marry on a sunny day in June.

Knock, knock.
Who's there?
Morton.
Morton who?
More turn to the right.

Knock, knock.
Who's there?
Oliver.
Oliver who?
A liver and bacon sandwich, please.

Knock, knock.
Who's there?
Othello.
Othello who?
A fellow I wouldn't trust an inch.

Knock, knock.
Who's there?
Paulina.
Paulina who?
Poor Lena is totally broke.

Knock, knock.
Who's there?
Puck.
Puck who?
Puck up all your belongings.

Knock, knock.
Who's there?
Toby.
Toby who?
To be or not to be.

Knock, knock.
Who's there?
Theseus.
Theseus who?
This useless idiot.

Knock, knock.
Who's there?
Thisbe.
Thisbe who?
This beef is too tough.

Knock, knock.
Who's there?
Vernon.
Vernon who?
Ver-non smokers only, this carriage.

Knock, knock.
Who's there?
Marsha.
Marsha who?
Martians have landed.

Knock, knock.
Who's there?
Maria.
Maria who?
Ma real name is Mary.

BONK!

OUCH!!

I'M SEEING STARS!!

CAREFUL YOU MARTIAN CLOT!

Knock, knock.
Who's there?
Abby.
Abby who?
Abby go lucky.

Knock, knock.
Who's there?
Adelaide.
Adelaide who?
'Ad 'e laid an egg, you would have been shocked.

Knock, knock.
Who's there?
Edie.
Edie who?
Edie come, edie go.

Knock, knock.
Who's there?
Adolph.
Adolph who?
A dolphin is an intelligent creature.

Knock, knock.
Who's there?
Sandy.
Sandy who?
'Sandeniably true.

Knock, knock.
Who's there?
Alfie.
Alfie who?
I'll feed the ducks if I want to.

Knock, knock.
Who's there?
Algie.
Algie who?
I'll gee up a slow horse.

Knock, knock.
Who's there?
Ellie.
Ellie who?
'Elicopters elevate vertically.

Knock, knock.
Who's there?
Elsie.
Elsie who?
I'll see you in my dreams.

Knock, knock.
Who's there?
Alphonse.
Alphonse who?
I'll fancy my chances of winning.

Knock, knock.
Who's there?
Ninette.
Ninette who?
Knee nettle-rash is irritating.

Knock, knock.
Who's there?
Nanette
Nanette who?
None ate any of it.

Knock, knock.
Who's there?
Augustine.
Augustine who?
August in Spain is too hot.

Knock, knock.
Who's there?
Belle.
Belle who?
Bell-bottom trousers for a sailor.

DONG!
DONG!

Knock, knock.
Who's there?
Bettina.
Bettina who?
Bet in a casino on roulette.

Knock, knock.
Who's there?
Benny.
Benny who?
Benny for your thoughts.

Knock, knock.
Who's there?
Bernardette.
Bernardette who?
Bernard ate more than was good for him.

Knock, knock.
Who's there?
Betty.
Betty who?
Betticoats should not show below dresses.

Knock, knock.
Who's there?
Biddy.
Biddy who?
Biddy you had to leave so early.

Knock, knock.
Who's there?
Brigid.
Brigid who?
Be rigid in your thoughts and standards.

Knock, knock.
Who's there?
Bronwen.
Bronwen who?
Brown when returning from holiday.

TWANG!

Knock, knock.
Who's there?
Bruce.
Bruce who?
Bruce easily with soft skin.

Knock, knock.
Who's there?
Bruno.
Bruno who?
Brew no more tea for me.

Knock, knock.
Who's there?
Katerina.
Katerina who?
Cater in a small house for a hundred guests.

Knock, knock.
Who's there?
Carlos.
Carlos who?
Carlossal cheek to do such a thing.

Knock, knock.
Who's there?
Carla.
Carla who?
Call 'er and she never hears.

Knock, knock.
Who's there?
Cosmo.
Cosmo who?
'Cos most people are like that.

Knock, knock.
Who's there?
Crispin.
Crispin who?
Crisp inside, soggy outside.

Knock, knock.
Who's there?
Tom Sawyer.
Tom Sawyer who?
Tom saw yer being naughty.

Knock, knock.
Who's there?
Delia.
Delia who?
Deal yer cards more openly.

Knock, knock.
Who's there?
Derek.
Derek who?
Directly across the road.

Knock, knock.
Who's there?
Dilys.
Dilys who?
Delicious food.

Knock, knock.
Who's there?
Donna.
Donna who?
Don a different hat for rainy days.

Knock, knock.
Who's there?
Eamon.
Eamon who?
Eamon to please at all times.

Knock, knock.
Who's there?
Doll.
Doll who?
Doll and wet all day.

Knock, knock.
Who's there?
Emrys.
Emrys who?
Emrisking everything for you.

Knock, knock.
Who's there?
Erasmus.
Erasmus who?
Errors must be corrected

Knock, knock.
Who's there?
Etta.
Etta who?
Ate a lot.

Knock, knock.
Who's there?
Rees.
Rees who?
Resembles a monkey.

Knock, knock.
Who's there?
Rex.
Rex who?
Wrecks may be full of sunken treasure.

Knock, knock.
Who's there?
Piers.
Piers who?
Peers through his specs.

Knock, knock.
Who's there?
Unwin.
Unwin who?
Unwinking with a glass eye.

Knock, knock.
Who's there?
Noel.
Noel who?
No elevator working.

Knock, knock.
Who's there?
Theresa.
Theresa who?
Trees are chopped up for firewood.

Knock, knock.
Who's there?
Thelma.
Thelma who?
Thel Ma I've gone to the shops.

Knock, knock.
Who's there?
Tabitha.
Tabitha who?
To beat 'er you'll have to cheat.

Knock, knock.
Who's there?
Sophia.
Sophia who?
So fear can cause panic.

Knock, knock.
Who's there?
Sonia.
Sonia who?
Sonia conscience if you lie.

Knock, knock.
Who's there?
Sheila.
Sheila who?
She lurks round corners

Knock, knock
Who's there?
Hermes.
Hermes who?
Her measles are very catching.

Knock, knock.
Who's there?
Shamus.
Shamus who?
Shame us into confessing.

Knock, knock.
Who's there?
Salome.
Salome who?
So loan me a fiver.

PLUCK!

Knock, knock.
Who's there?
Rolf.
Rolf who?
Roll for a six on the dice.

Knock, knock.
Who's there?
Rodney.
Rodney who?
Rod needed for fisherman.

Knock, knock.
Who's there?
Gary.
Gary who?
Gary on, sergeant-major.

Knock, knock.
Who's there?
Sheena.
Sheena who?
Sheen a pair of shocks lying around?

Knock, knock.
Who's there?
Ira
Ira who?
'Ire a car and drive yourself

Knock, knock.
Who's there?
Jonas.
Jonas who?
Joe gnashing his teeth with fury.

Knock, knock.
Who's there?
Justus.
Justus who?
Just as bad-tempered as ever.

Knock, knock.
Who's there?
Lois.
Lois who?
Lowest of the low.

Knock, knock.
Who's there?
Lucas.
Lucas who?
Look as sweet as you can.

Knock, knock.
Who's there?
Rod Stewart.
Rod Stewart who?
Rod's too artful by half.

Knock, knock.
Who's there?
Narcissus.
Narcissus who?
Now scissors are much safer than a penknife.

Knock, knock.
Who's there?
Paulus.
Paulus who?
Paul us another couple of pints.

Knock, knock.
Who's there?
Perry.
Perry who?
Perilously close to the rocks.

Knock, knock.
Who's there?
Sarah.
Sarah who?
Sarah doctor in the house?

Knock, knock.
Who's there?
Shadrach.
Shadrach who?
She'd wreck any car the way she drives!

Knock, knock.
Who's there?
Sheba.
Sheba who?
Cheaper if you buy large quantities.

Knock, knock.
Who's there?
Zachary.
Zachary who?
Zachary, dackery, duck, ducks do often quack.

HOW AM I DOING?

Knock, knock.
Who's there?
Monro.
Monro who?
Man rowing in a boat.

Knock, knock.
Who's there?
Aunt.
Aunt who?
Aren't your eyes a beautiful blue?

Knock, knock.
Who's there?
Uncle.
Uncle who?
Uncalled for remarks.

Knock, knock.
Who's there?
Blake.
Blake who?
Blake and white.

Knock, knock.
Who's there?
Drake.
Drake who?
Drake the leaves off the lawn?

Knock, knock.
Who's there?
Scott.
Scott who?
Scott to be a better way of doing this.

Knock, knock.
Who's there?
Fraser.
Fraser who?
Fraser jolly good fellow.

Knock, knock.
Who's there?
Howard.
Howard who?
How 'ard are diamonds?

Knock, knock.
Who's there?
Seymour.
Seymour who?
Seymour if you stand on the wall.

Knock, knock.
Who's there?
Warren.
Warren who?
War and Peace by Tolstoy.

Knock, knock.
Who's there?
Duff.
Duff who?
Duffeningly loud music in my ears.

Knock, knock.
Who's there?
Serge.
Serge who?
Search high and low.

Knock, knock.
Who's there?
Conway.
Conway who?
Conway off the beaten track.

Knock, knock.
Who's there?
Hudson.
Hudson who?
Had sons and daughters.

Knock, knock.
Who's there?
Mungo Park.
Mungo Park who?
Mum go park on yellow lines?

Knock, knock.
Who's there?
Lewis.
Lewis who?
Lewis form of human life.

Knock, knock.
Who's there?
Davis.
Davis who?
Day visitors and night callers.

Knock, knock.
Who's there?
Mister.
Mister who?
Missed a bus and had to walk.

Knock, knock.
Who's there?
Harris.
Harris who?
Harassed by people claiming money.

Knock, knock.
Who's there?
Murray.
Murray who?
Murray Christmas to one and all!

Knock, knock.
Who's there?
Wilson.
Wilson who?
Will Sonia be among the guests?

Knock, knock.
Who's there?
Bradley.
Bradley who?
Bradley in need of repair.

Knock, knock.
Who's there?
Brock.
Brock who?
Brockfast in bed.

Knock, knock.
Who's there?
Russell.
Russell who?
Rustle of a bustle on an old dress.

Knock, knock.
Who's there?
Lester.
Lester who?
Less turkey, more chicken.

Knock, knock.
Who's there?
Dali.
Dali who?
Dali papers and weekly magazines.

Knock, knock.
Who's there?
Watt.
Watt who?
Watt a carry-on!

Knock, knock.
Who's there?
Brett.
Brett who?
Bretter late than never.

Knock, knock.
Who's there?
Lenin.
Lenin who?
Linen should not be washed in public.

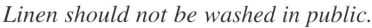

SHATTERED
UNDIES

Knock, knock.
Who's there?
Cohen.
Cohen who?
Cohen, cohen, gone.

Knock, knock.
Who's there?
Giles.
Giles who?
Child's play, that's what it is.

Knock, knock.
Who's there?
Odette.
Odette who?
A debt I can't pay

Knock, knock.
Who's there?
Archer.
Archer who?
Are churns still used to put milk in?

ALL THAT KNOCKY KNOCK-KNOCK'S GIVEN ME BONCE ACHE